States

DELAWARE

by Jason Kirchner

CAPSTONE PRESS
a capstone imprint

Next Page Books are published by Capstone Press,
1710 Roe Crest Drive, North Mankato, Minnesota 56003
www.mycapstone.com

Library of Congress Cataloging-in-Publication Data
Cataloging-in-publication information is on file with the Library of Congress.
ISBN 978-1-5157-0394-5 (library binding)
ISBN 978-1-5157-0454-6 (paperback)
ISBN 978-1-5157-0506-2 (ebook PDF)

Editorial Credits
Jaclyn Jaycox, editor; Richard Korab and Katy LaVigne, designers; Morgan Walters, media researcher; Laura Manthe, production specialist

Photo Credits
Capstone Press: Angi Gahler, map 4, 7; Corbis: Bettmann, 28; Dreamstime: Americanspirit, 25, Georgios Kollidas, 26; Getty Images: 4X5 Coll-Devaney, 12, Hulton Archive, middle 19; iStockphoto: roc8jas, 10; Library of Congress: Prints and Photographs Division, bottom 18, Prints and Photographs Division/J.E. Miller, K.C., middle 18; Newscom: DEA / R. APPIANI Universal Images Group, middle left 21, Everett Collection, top 19, JONATHAN ERNST/REUTERS, 29; One Mile Up, Inc., flag, seal 23; Shutterstock: bibiphoto, bottom 24, Bruce Goerlitz Photo, 7, CatbirdHill, top left 20, Christian Hoiberg, 9, Colin D. Young, bottom left 8, Denis Tabler, bottom right 21, Everett Historical, 27, Fotokostic, top 24, Greg Kushmerek, middle right 21, hutch photography, 16, Jason and Bonnie Grower, top 18, Jon Bilous, bottom right 8, Joseph Sohm, 5, 17, KumikoMurakamiCampos, bottom right 20, Leena Robinson, top right 21, Nagel Photography, 13, PeterVrabel, bottom left 20, Pixeljoy, bottom left 21, s_bukley, bottom 19, Songquan Deng, cover, T.Dallas, top left 21, TMsara, 14, vahalla, 6, Vasilius, top right 20; Wikimedia: Littleinfo, 15, Smallbones, 11

All design elements by Shutterstock

Printed and bound in China.
0316/CA21600187
012016 009436F16

TABLE OF CONTENTS

Want to take your research further? Ask your librarian if your school subscribes to PebbleGo Next. If so, when you see this helpful symbol throughout the book, log onto www.pebblegonext.com for bonus downloads and information.

LOCATION

Delaware faces the Atlantic Ocean. It's a tiny state. Only Rhode Island is smaller. Delaware is located on a piece of land called the Delmarva Peninsula. Delaware, Maryland, and Virginia all share this peninsula. Maryland borders Delaware on the south and west. To the north is Pennsylvania. Delaware's border with Pennsylvania is famous. It's a perfect arc, or section of a circle. No other border in the country is shaped this way. Dover, the state capital, is in the center of the state. Dover, Wilmington, Newark, and Middletown are the state's biggest cities.

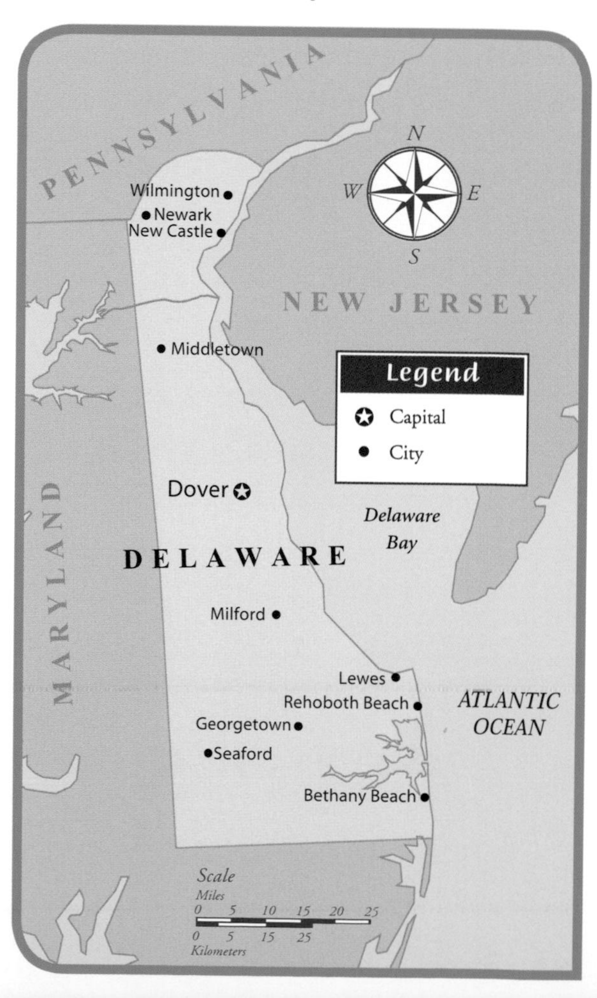

PebbleGo Next Bonus! To print and label your own map, go to www.pebblegonext.com and search keywords:

DE MAP

Wilmington is the most populated city in Delaware.

GEOGRAPHY

Almost all of Delaware is part of a larger area of land called the Atlantic Coastal Plain. It's a region of farmland, forests, and streams. Far northern Delaware is in the Piedmont region. It has forested hills and river valleys. Most of Delaware is flat and close to sea level. In the southeastern part of the state lies Cape Henlopen State Park. The Great Cypress Swamp is in southern Delaware. Delaware's highest point is in New Castle County in northern Delaware. This point is 450 feet (137 meters) above sea level.

PebbleGo Next Bonus! To watch a video about the Migratory Bird Festival, go to www.pebblegonext.com and search keywords:

DE VIDEO

The Great Cypress Swamp is the largest freshwater wetland in Delaware.

Cape Henlopen State Park is located along the Atlantic coast.
Legend
Highest Point
Point of Interest
River
Christina River
Delaware River
Chesapeake and Delaware Canal
Delaware Bay
N
E
S
W
ATLANTIC OCEAN
Cape Henlopen
Rehoboth Bay
Great Cypress Swamp
Scale
Miles
0 5 10 15 20 25
0 5 15 25
Kilometers

WEATHER

Delaware's weather is mild along the coast. Farther inland, temperatures vary. The average summer temperature is 74 degrees Fahrenheit (23 degrees Celsius). The average winter temperature is 35°F (2°C).

Average High and Low Temperatures (Dover, DE)

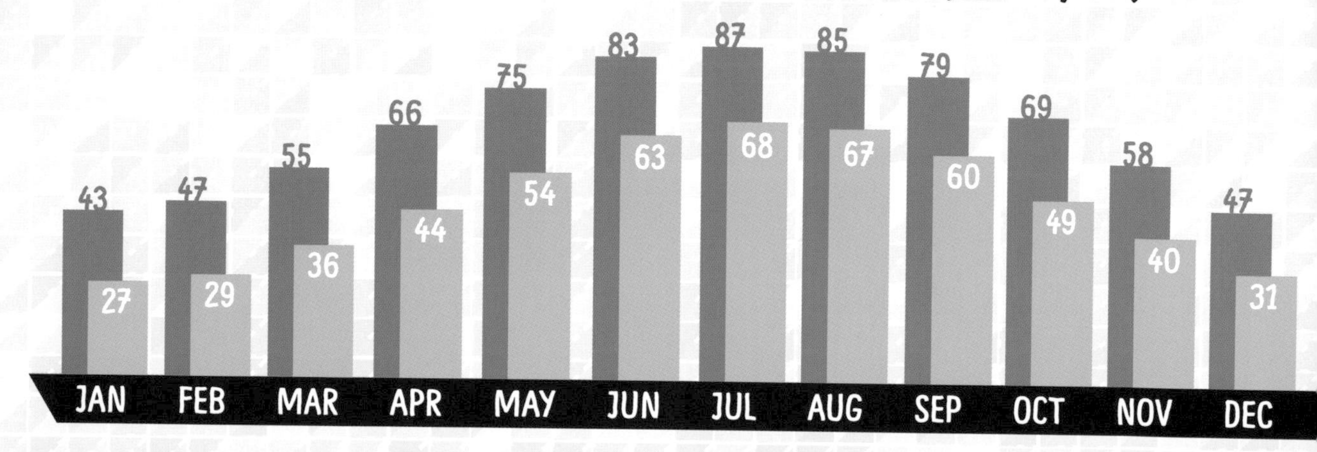

LANDMARKS

Rehoboth Beach

Rehoboth Beach is one of Delaware's most popular beaches. It lies along the Rehoboth Bay in the southeastern part of the state. Thousands of people come to Rehoboth Beach to walk along the boardwalk, relax on the beach, or play sports.

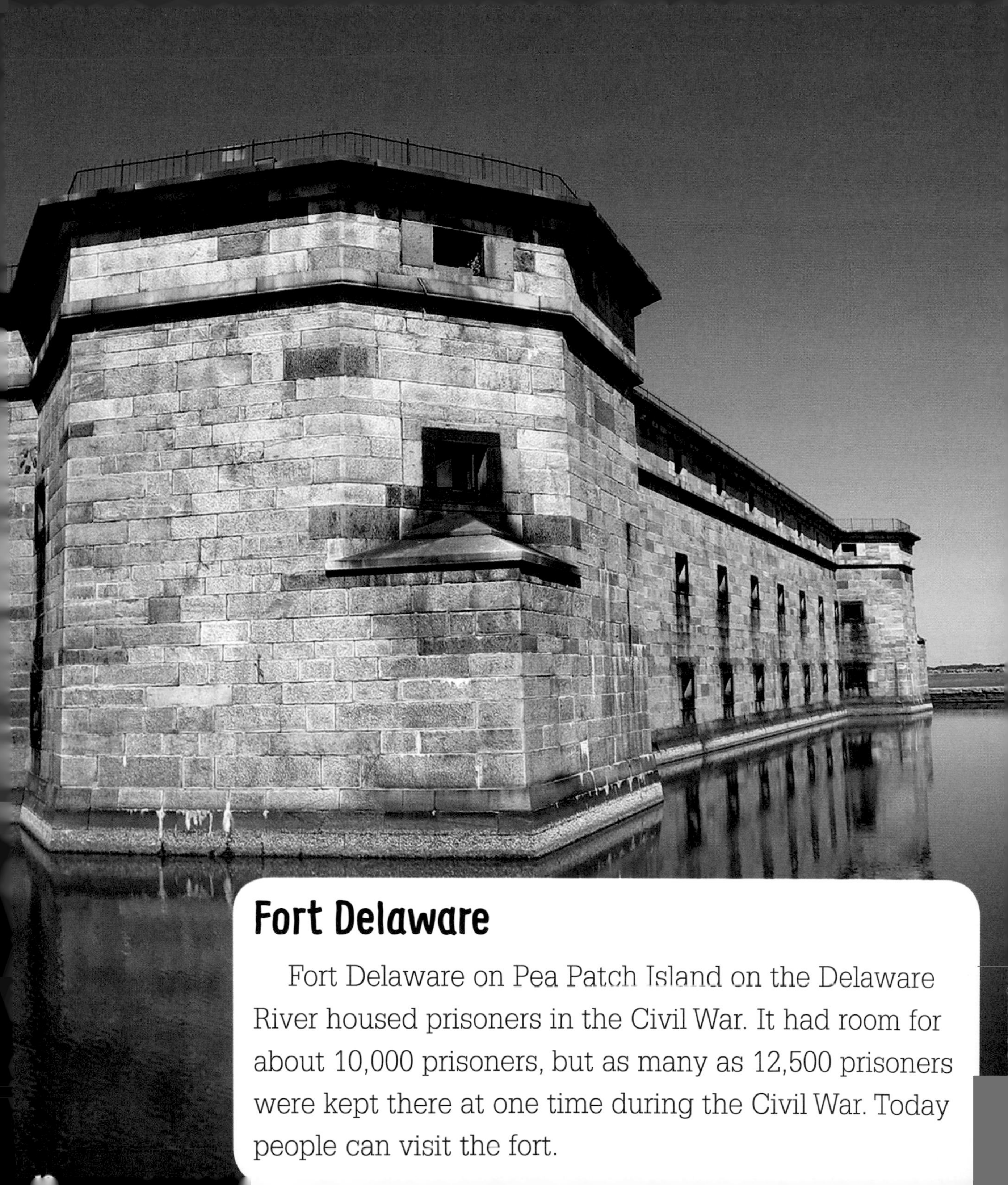

Fort Delaware

Fort Delaware on Pea Patch Island on the Delaware River housed prisoners in the Civil War. It had room for about 10,000 prisoners, but as many as 12,500 prisoners were kept there at one time during the Civil War. Today people can visit the fort.

Zwaanendael Museum

The Zwaanendael Museum in Lewes in southern Delaware honors the state's first settlement, founded by the Dutch in 1631. The museum is built like a Dutch town hall. It houses objects used by American Indians and early settlers.

HISTORY AND GOVERNMENT

While on a quest to find a northeastern passage to China, Henry Hudson discovered the Delaware Bay.

Delaware was once home to thousands of American Indians, including the Lenape and the Nanticoke. In 1609 British explorer Henry Hudson sailed into Delaware Bay. The Delaware region changed hands many times. In 1638 Swedish settlers built Fort Christina near present-day Wilmington. In 1655 the Dutch took over the region. The British seized the area in 1664. In 1682 William Penn was given present-day Delaware. Delaware soldiers joined the other American colonists in the Revolutionary War (1775–1783). The colonists won their freedom from Great Britain in 1783. Delaware became the first U.S. state in 1787.

Delaware's state government has three branches. The governor leads the executive branch. The legislature makes the state laws. It is made up of the 21-member Senate and the 41-member House of Representatives. Delaware's judges and courts are the judicial branch. They uphold the laws.

Delaware's state capitol building is located in Dover.

INDUSTRY

Delaware may be small, but it's one of the nation's most industrial states. Chemicals are Delaware's top factory products. They include nylon, paint, dyes, and chemicals made from petroleum. Delaware's DuPont company is the nation's largest chemical company. One of Delaware's leading industries is finance. Many banks and credit card companies are in Wilmington.

Farmland covers about 40 percent of Delaware's land. Soybeans are the top crop. Delaware's farmers grow corn, wheat,

A majority of the soybeans grown in Delaware are used for animal feed.

potatoes, peas, peaches, and apples. Broilers, which are young chickens, are Delaware's most valuable farm product. Most of Delaware's broilers come from Sussex County.

Service industries make up about 90 percent of Delaware's jobs. Many service workers are in the banking industry. Others work in restaurants, stores, hospitals, or schools.

The DuPont headquarters is located in Wilmington.

POPULATION

Many ethnic groups make Delaware their home. Most of Delaware's population is white. Many live in the central and southern part of the state. About 20 percent of Delaware's residents are African-Americans. Other people in Delaware have Hispanic, Asian, or American Indian backgrounds. Hispanics make up about 8 percent of the state's residents. About 3 percent of Delaware's residents are Asian. A small tribe of Nanticoke Indians lives in southern Delaware. Delaware also has a small population of Amish people. This religious group believes in living a simple life. Most of Delaware's Amish population lives in Kent County in central Delaware.

Population by Ethnicity

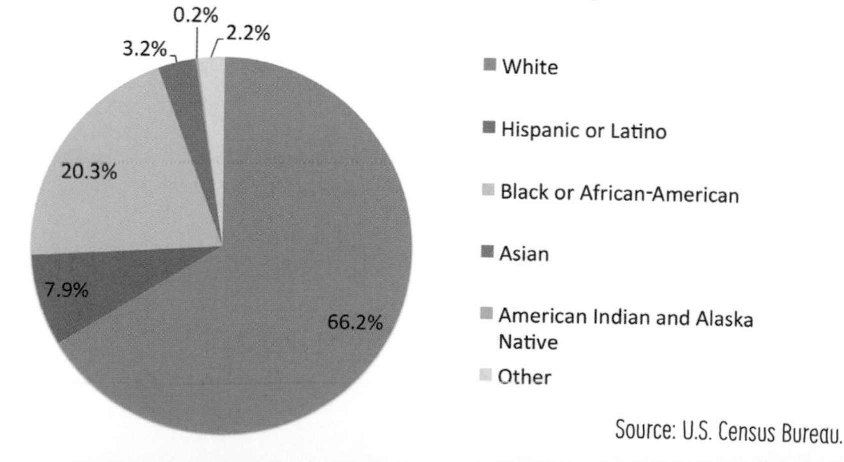

Source: U.S. Census Bureau.

RACE
MOTORCROSS

FAMOUS PEOPLE

Joseph Biden Jr. (1942–) was elected vice president of the United States in 2008. He was re-elected in 2012. Biden represented Delaware in the U.S. Senate from 1973 to 2008. He was only 30 when he won the Senate seat in 1973. He was the youngest senator elected in U.S. history. He was born in Pennsylvania and later moved to Wilmington.

William Julius (Judy) Johnson (1899–1989) was a Negro Leagues baseball player famous for his game-winning hits. He was born in Maryland and grew up in Wilmington. He is in the National Baseball Hall of Fame.

Thomas Garrett (1789–1871) was an antislavery activist. He helped more than 2,000 slaves escape through the Underground Railroad, which was a system that helped slaves in the South reach freedom in the North. He was born in Pennsylvania and later moved to Wilmington.

John Phillips Marquand (1893–1960) wrote novels about wealthy New Englanders. He won the 1937 Pulitzer Prize for his novel *The Late George Apley*. He was born in Wilmington.

Annie Jump Cannon (1863–1941) was an astronomer. She discovered more than 300 stars. She also compiled a catalog of more than 200,000 stars. She was born in Dover.

Elisabeth Shue (1963–) is an actress. Her movies include *The Karate Kid* (1984), *Leaving Las Vegas* (1995), *The Hollow Man* (2000), and *Hope Springs* (2012). She was born in Wilmington.

STATE SYMBOLS

Tree

American holly

Flower

peach blossom

Bird

blue hen chicken

Fish

weakfish

PebbleGo Next Bonus! To make a dessert using a popular fruit in Delaware, go to www.pebblegonext.com and search keywords:

DE RECIPE

Marine Animal

horseshoe crab

Butterfly

tiger swallowtail

Mineral

sillimanite

Herb

sweet goldenrod

Fossil

belemnite

Insect

ladybug

FAST FACTS

STATEHOOD
1787

CAPITAL ☆
Dover

LARGEST CITY •
Wilmington

SIZE
1,949 square miles (5,048 square kilometers)
land area (2010 U.S. Census Bureau)

POPULATION
925,749 (2013 U.S. Census estimate)

STATE NICKNAME
The First State

STATE MOTTO
"Liberty and Independence"

STATE SEAL

Delaware's state seal shows the coat of arms with agricultural symbols of a farmer, an ox, wheat, and corn. The Revolutionary War soldier represents the importance of the men who fought for Delaware's rights. The ship and the water represent the importance of the rivers and ocean to Delaware's economy. Under the farmer and soldier is a banner with the state motto, "Liberty and Independence." The seal also shows three dates, 1793, 1847, and 1907. The seal was changed in these years. The state seal was adopted on January 17, 1777.

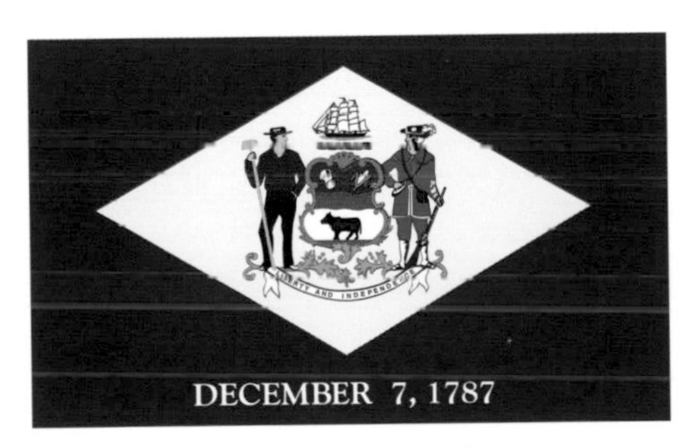

PebbleGo Next Bonus!
To print and color your own flag, go to www.pebblegonext.com and search keywords:

STATE FLAG

Delaware's state flag is blue with a gold diamond in the center. Inside the diamond is the state coat of arms, which shows a ship, a farmer, and a Revolutionary War soldier. Below the diamond is the date December 7, 1787, which is the date that Delaware signed the Constitution. It was the first state to do so. The flag's design was adopted on July 24, 1913.

MINING PRODUCTS

magnesium, sand and gravel

MANUFACTURED GOODS

chemicals, food products, petroleum and coal products, computer and electronic equipment, plastic and rubber products, paper

FARM PRODUCTS

chickens, soybeans, wheat, corn, vegetables, milk, peaches

PebbleGo Next Bonus! To learn the lyrics to the state song, go to www.pebblegonext.com and search keywords:

DE SONG

DELAWARE TIMELINE

1609 English explorer Henry Hudson, hired by a Dutch company, sails into Delaware Bay.

1620 The Pilgrims establish a colony in the New World in present-day Massachusetts.

1631 Dutch settlers found Zwaanendael in southern Delaware, where Lewes is today. Lenape Indians kill almost all the settlers.

1638 Settlers from Sweden build Fort Christina near present-day Wilmington. This is Delaware's first permanent European settlement. The settlers plan to trade goods with American Indians.

1682

Englishman William Penn takes over the land that later becomes Delaware.

1775–1783

Colonists fight for independence from Great Britain in the Revolutionary War.

1777

British troops invade Delaware during the Revolutionary War, beating the colonists in the Battle of Cooch's Bridge near Newark. It is the only Revolutionary War battle fought in Delaware.

1787

Delaware becomes the first U.S. state on December 7.

1802

Frenchman Éleuthère Irénée du Pont opens a gunpowder mill on Brandywine Creek near Wilmington. Du Pont's business grows into a successful chemical industry.

1861–1865

The Union and the Confederacy fight the Civil War. Delaware fights with the Union.

1892

Delaware receives a small piece of land called The Wedge from Maryland.

1939–1945

World War II is fought; the United States enters the war in 1941.

1951

The Delaware Memorial Bridge opens, connecting Delaware and New Jersey.

1963

Delaware Turnpike opens, completing a nonstop highway between Boston, Massachusetts, and Washington, D.C. It is later renamed the John F. Kennedy Memorial Highway.

1971

Delaware passes the Coastal Zone Act, which bans industrial plants along the coast.

1987

Delaware residents celebrate the 200th birthday of their state.

2000 Ruth Ann Minner is elected Delaware's first female governor.

2008 Longtime U.S. senator Joe Biden of Delaware is elected vice president of the United States. Barack Obama is elected president.

2012 Hurricane Sandy strikes the eastern United States on October 29. The storm causes strong winds, flooding, and billions of dollars of damage. Delaware receives more than $2 million in federal aid to recover from the storm.

2015 Delaware receives the first state-level Health Champion award from the American Diabetes Association.

Glossary

chemical *(KE-muh-kuhl)*—a substance used in or produced by chemistry; medicines, gunpowder, and food preservatives are all made from chemicals

executive *(ig-ZE-kyuh-tiv)*—the branch of government that makes sure laws are followed

industry *(IN-duh-stree)*—a business which produces a product or provides a service

inland *(IN-luhnd)*—away from the ocean

invade *(in-VADE)*—to send armed forces into another country in order to take it over

judicial *(joo-DISH-uhl)*—the branch of government that explains and interprets the laws

legislature *(LEJ-iss-lay-chur)*—a group of elected officials who have the power to make or change laws for a country or state

peninsula *(puh-NIN-suh-luh)*—a piece of land that is surrounded by water on three sides

permanent *(PUR-muh-nuhnt)*—lasting for a long time or forever

petroleum *(puh-TROH-lee-uhm)*—an oily liquid found below the earth's surface used to make gasoline, heating oil, and many other products

region *(REE-juhn)*—a large area

Read More

Dillard, Sheri. *What's Great About Delaware?* Our Great States. Minneapolis: Lerner Publications, 2015.

Ganeri, Anita. *United States of America: A Benjamin Blog and His Inquisitive Dog Guide.* Country Guides. Chicago: Heinemann Raintree, 2015.

King, David. *Delaware.* It's My State! New York: Cavendish Square Publishing, 2015.

Internet Sites

FactHound offers a safe, fun way to find Internet sites related to this book. All of the sites on FactHound have been researched by our staff.

Here's all you do:

Visit *www.facthound.com*

Type in this code: 9781515703945

Check out projects, games and lots more at
www.capstonekids.com

Critical Thinking Using the Common Core

1. Delaware is a tiny state. Are there any other states smaller than Delaware? Which one(s)? (Key Ideas and Details)
2. Rehoboth Beach is one of the most popular beaches in Delaware. Looking at the map on page 4, where would you find this beach? (Key Ideas and Details)
3. Delaware has a small population of Amish people. The Amish believe in living a simple life. What does a simple life mean to you? What could you give up to make your life simpler? (Integration of Knowledge and Ideas)

Index